The *Little Book of* PRINCE EDWARD ISLAND

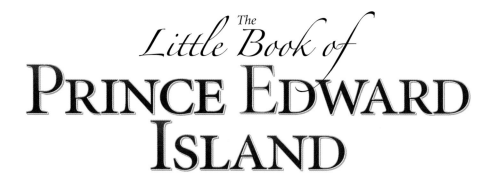

JOHN SYLVESTER

ACORNPRESS

Charlottetown—2011

Cover and interior design by
Troy Cole—Envision Graphic Design

Printed and bound in China

DEDICATION
To the members and supporters of the L. M.
Montgomery Land Trust — working to preserve
the scenic agricultural and coastal landscape
on Prince Edward Island's north shore.

ACKNOWLEDGMENTS —
Special thanks to the Mi'Kmaq Confederacy
of Prince Edward Island, David Hardy,
Tourism Prince Edward Island, Laurie Brinklow,
Rachel, Katelyn and Dianne.

Canadä

The Canada Council | Le Conseil des Arts
for the Arts | du Canada

The publisher acknowledges the support of the
Government of Canada through the Canada
Book Fund of the Department of Canadian
Heritage and the Canada Council for the Arts
Block Grant Program.

ACORNPRESS

P.O. Box 22024
Charlottetown, Prince Edward Island
C1A 9J2

acornpresscanada.com

Library and Archives Canada Cataloguing in Publication

Sylvester, John, 1955-

The little book of Prince Edward Island / John Sylvester.

ISBN 978-1-894838-59-7

1. Prince Edward Island--Pictorial works. I. Title.

FC2612.S95 2011   971.7'050222   C2011-900717-7

Introduction

Prince Edward Island is a wonderful place for a landscape photographer. When I arrived on the Island almost thirty years ago, I was immediately drawn to the rural and coastal landscape with its vivid palette of primary colours: red cliffs, green fields, and blue waters. The singular visual character of the Island is shaped not only by geography, but also by the farmers and fishers who derive their living from land and sea. While much has changed during the past three decades – small farms have disappeared, fishing communities have dwindled, and a proliferation of houses along the fragile coastline have obscured what were once pristine ocean views – I continue to be inspired by the unique tapestry of the Island. There is no place like it, anywhere.

My Island photography "season" mimics that of farmers and fishers. When farmers take to the land in their tractors – dragging planters across dusty fields – and fishers begin hauling lobster traps in the Gulf of St. Lawrence, I venture forth to record the first signs of an Island spring. My days may be just as long as those who toil on land and sea. I rise early to catch the first rays of morning sunlight and stay late to witness the last light of day.

Summer brings frantic activity as I try to capture as much of the Island's most beautiful – but all too brief – season. It's a time for wildflowers, misty mornings, fields of round hay bales, blossom-covered potato fields, golden fields of canola, and, of course, the beach – the main attraction for summer visitors and Islanders alike. There's nothing I like better than to conclude an evening of photography at a North Shore beach, feeling the sand between my toes and watching the sun dissolve into the waters of the Gulf of St. Lawrence.

Autumn brings its own activity with the harvest – on both the land and the water. Fields turn from green to gold with the ripening of grain crops; potato fields are laid bare once again; marram grass on coastal dunes takes on an amber hue with the first frost. Autumn ends with a technicolour display of leaves along canopied country roads and wooded hillsides.

Winter is a quieter time, but when the first snow falls in late December or early January, I'm anxious to venture forth once again with camera in hand. Winter's beauty is fleeting on Prince Edward Island, so I must take advantage of every snowfall, "silver freeze," and ice storm that I can.

The collection of images on these pages is the result of my most recent efforts to convey the beauty and spirit of this special place that continues to inspire me.

ABOVE ∻ Foxes are plentiful in Prince Edward Island and are often observed in fields, roadsides, and coastal dunes. I spotted this vixen hunting for mice in an overgrown field. Upon hearing the sound of my camera shutter she bounded over to investigate, "posing" briefly for this portrait.

FACING PAGE ∻ Canola is a relatively new crop in Prince Edward Island, but bright fields of the oilseed are now a common sight in mid-July. Here a golden carpet of canola blossoms stretches down to the sea past an old farmhouse in Guernsey Cove.

RIGHT ∾ A canopy of
altocumulus clouds
drifts over a Mayfield
farmhouse.

ABOVE ∿ These horses in Sea View were much too busy enjoying lush summer pasture to pay any attention to the photographer.

FACING PAGE ∿ Cows are naturally curious. So when I stop to photograph them grazing contentedly in a field, they'll often amble over to investigate, which sometimes spoils the picture I was trying to make! In this case, however, it made for a more interesting composition.

OVERLEAF ∿ A newly planted potato field resembles a blanket of corduroy stretching down to the dunes at South Lake, near the eastern tip of the Island.

RIGHT ∾ After the harvest, windrows of canola straw are left lying in a field overlooking Northumberland Strait at Guernsey Cove.

OVERLEAF ∾ Coastal cliffs glow red from the setting sun at Cape Wolfe on the Island's western shore.

LEFT ∾ There's no parallel parking in Malpeque Harbour! Lobster boats are tied gunwale to gunwale with bows pointed seaward, ready for launching.

ABOVE ∾ The setting sun casts long shadows across coastal farmland at Cousins Shore.

FACING PAGE ∾ Straw bales await collection after the grain harvest amid Brookfield's gently rolling hills.

OVERLEAF ∾ A Hampshire farmhouse is highlighted by evening sunlight against a dramatic backdrop of storm clouds.

PREVIOUS PAGE ~ The soft sandstone cliffs of Cavendish (left) and Sea View (right) are easily eroded and sculpted into fanciful formations by ocean waves. The Island coastline loses up to a metre a year to erosion.

ABOVE ∾ At the western end of the Island, West Point lighthouse overlooks the dunes and beach at Cedar Dunes Provincial Park. The lighthouse has been converted to an inn and guests can stay in rooms located in the lighthouse tower.

FACING PAGE ∾ The Souris lighthouse stands sentinel overlooking the town's harbour and Colville Bay.

Above ❧ Ready for Halloween, piles of pumpkins await buyers at a farm market in St. Eleanors.

Facing Page ❧ Autumn leaves provide a colourful backdrop to this tidy farmstead located on the Blue Shank Road.

RIGHT ∾ "Mist in the hollow, fine day to follow" is a common Island expression. This mist-shrouded scene in Darlington soon gave way to sunny skies.

ABOVE ∿ This scene at Springbrook – in this case, across a blossom-flecked potato field to New London Bay, Cavendish sandspit, and the Gulf of St. Lawrence – is one of my favourite Island viewscapes.

LEFT ∿ This view of farm fields and ocean at Park Corner exemplifies the colours of an Island summer with its multiple shades of green and blue.

ABOVE ~ A lone kayaker enjoys a reflective autumn paddle along the Bonshaw River.

RIGHT ~ A canopy of colour awaits all who venture along the Island's heritage roads in October. This is the Princetown-Warburton road near Millvale.

PREVIOUS PAGE ~ Cape Tryon lighthouse stands atop the Island's highest coastal cliffs, commanding a spectacular view of the Gulf of St. Lawrence.

ABOVE ∾ Hockey players enjoy a game of "shinny" on frozen Dalvay Pond below stately Dalvay-by-the-Sea Hotel, a "summer only" inn.

FACING PAGE ∾ Long December nights in the country are brightened by Christmas lights such as these on a farmhouse in Breadalbane.

RIGHT ∿ An early winter snowfall blankets the rolling hills of North Wiltshire. The late afternoon sun appeared briefly during the snowfall, creating the weather phenomena I've dubbed "sun-flurries."

ABOVE ∾ Fragrant apple blossoms and a tractor working the land embody the sights, sounds, and smells of an Island spring.

FACING PAGE ∾ Neat rows of newly planted potatoes trace the hills near Crapuad.

ABOVE ∼ A white lupin stands alone amongst surrounding blossoms of purple and pink.

FACING PAGE ∼ A country road in Clinton is resplendent with a profusion of colourful lupin blossoms.

RIGHT ∽ St. Mary's Church in Indian River, built in 1902, was designed by prominent Island architect William Critchlow Harris. Today it is home to the Indian River Festival, an internationally renowned summer music festival.

ABOVE ∾ Blockhouse Point light stands sentry at the entrance to Charlottetown Harbour. Established in 1851, it is the second-oldest lighthouse in Prince Edward Island.

FACING PAGE ∾ The beautifully restored Bagnall's Mill in Hunter River is reminiscent of simpler times in rural Prince Edward Island.

OVERLEAF LEFT ∾ The first snowfall of winter graces a timeless scene in Wheatley River.

OVERLEAF RIGHT ∾ A rare combination of new snow and morning mist settle over the tree-lined hills of North Wiltshire.

ABOVE ∾ A colourful display of traditional wooden lobster buoys decorate a shed in the fishing village of North Rustico.

FACING PAGE ∾ Oyster fisher David Hardy of Bideford holds a crate of freshly harvested "choice" Island oysters.

PREVIOUS PAGE ∾ On a misty September morning dozens of oyster fishers descend upon the West River with their dories and long-handled tongs to harvest the popular shellfish.

Above ∾ A fishing boat and tidy sheds reflect in the calm waters of Bay Fortune.

Facing Page ∾ The massive blades of these turbines are stilled on a windless summer evening at West Cape. Power-generating wind turbines like these have been erected at several locations across the Island.

Above ≁ On a clear October morning, a solitary horse grazes on pasture overlooking Northumberland Strait, near High Bank.

Right ≁ A fishing boat crosses New London Bay framed by the dunes of Cavendish sandspit and the rolling cropland of Springbrook.

Overleaf Left ≁ The windswept dunes of Prince Edward Island National Park provide an ever-changing scene for the photographer. I'm always excited to see the wind's latest creation.

Overleaf Right ≁ Cyclists enjoy a summer outing on the bicycle path in Charlottetown's Victoria Park.

ABOVE AND FACING PAGE ᔋ Green Gables House in Cavendish – a National Historic Site – is acknowledged as the inspiration for the setting of Lucy Maud Montgomery's most famous book, *Anne of Green Gables*.

ABOVE ∾ A black-capped chickadee balances on an icy perch in the aftermath of a freezing-rain storm.

LEFT ∾ A red fox, resplendent in its winter coat of lustrous thick fur, pauses at the forest edge in Prince Edward Island National Park.

ABOVE ᔚ Prince Edward Island boasts the largest population of Great Blue Herons in Atlantic Canada. While herons typically are sighted patrolling the Island's marshes and shoreline, this individual chose an unusual vantage point from which to survey the view.

FACING PAGE ᔚ Visitors enjoy a summer evening on Cavendish Beach in Prince Edward Island National Park.

ABOVE ∻ The exquisite blossoms of the Showy Lady's Slipper are much less common than the provincial floral emblem, the Pink Lady's Slipper, but can be found in forest locations throughout Prince Edward Island.

FACING PAGE ∻ A profusion of phlox flowers blossom along the shore at Bayview on New London Bay.

ABOVE ∾ A lobster boat laden with traps leaves North Rustico Harbour on "Setting Day," the opening day of the spring lobster fishing season.

FACING PAGE ∾ A full moon rises above New London Harbour lighthouse and the ice-covered Gulf of St. Lawrence in late March.

ABOVE ⁓ Autumn storms loosen Irish Moss, a seaweed harvested using horses dragging cage-like rakes through the surf. A substance called carageenan is extracted from the moss for use as a thickener in ice cream, toothpaste, and various other products.

FACING PAGE ⁓ Waves pound the shore at Cape Turner in Prince Edward Island National Park.

ABOVE ∾ In June, lupins blossom in abundance along the Island's rural roads, signalling the arrival of summer.

FACING PAGE ∾ Hay bales randomly scattered across a field in Long River will be gathered up to provide winter feed for dairy cattle.

OVERLEAF ∾ Still waters in New London Bay reflect a tranquil view of Stanley Bridge.

Left ∿ The thirteen-kilometre-long Confederation Bridge has joined Prince Edward Island to mainland Canada since 1997, but we still call ourselves "Islanders."

Previous Page Left ∿ In Prince Edward Island National Park a wind-scoured dune and scudding clouds frame a view of the Gulf of St. Lawrence.

Previous Page Right ∿ On my way to the beach on an August afternoon I couldn't resist stopping to photograph these feathered cirrus clouds above Covehead lighthouse.

Overleaf ∿ The spectacular offshore wilderness of Hog Island – a Mi'Kmaq Heritage Landscape – stretches for more than fifteen kilometres across the mouth of Malpeque Bay.